Sacagawea

SPIRIT
of America®

Sacagawea

NATIVE AMERICAN INTERPRETER

By Judy Alter

The Child's World®
Chanhassen, Minnesota

7

Sacagawea

Published in the United States of America by The Child's World®
PO Box 326 • Chanhassen, MN 55317-0326 • 800-599-READ • www.childsworld.com

Acknowledgments
The Child's World®: Mary Berendes, Publishing Director

Editorial Directions, Inc.: E. Russell Primm, Emily Dolbear, and Lucia Raatma, Editors; Linda S. Koutris, Photo Selector; Dawn Friedman, Photo Research; Red Line Editorial, Fact Research; Irene Keller, Copy Editor; Tim Griffin/IndexServ, Indexer; Chad Rubel, Proofreader

Photos
The Newark Museum, Newark, NJ/Art Resource: 15 top; Royal Geographical Society, London, UK/Bridgeman Art Library: 14; Academy of Natural Sciences of Philadelphia/Corbis: 9; Bettmann/Corbis: 13; Michael T. Sedam/Corbis: 16; Lee Snider/Corbis: 18; Macduff Everton/Corbis: 28; Hulton Archive/Getty Images: 15 bottom, 24; Library of Congress: 23, 25; Missouri Historical Society, St. Louis: 21; North Wind Picture Archives: cover, 6, 7, 8, 10, 11, 20; Oregon Historical Society: 22 top (#OrHi 87523), 22 bottom (#OrHi 76334); Stock Montage: 2, 27.

Registration

Library of Congress Cataloging-in-Publication Data
Alter, Judy, 1938–
  Sacagawea : Native American interpreter / by Judy Alter.
    p. cm.
  Summary: A biography of the Shoshoni Indian woman who played an
  important role in guiding the Lewis and Clark expedition through the
  Northwest Territory of the United States in 1805-1806.
  Includes bibliographical references (p.) and index.
   ISBN 1-56766-166-1 (library bound : alk. paper)
  1. Sacagawea, 1786–1884—Juvenile literature. 2. Lewis and Clark
  Expedition (1804–1806)—Juvenile literature. 3. Shoshoni
  women—Biography—Juvenile literature. 4. Shoshoni
  Indians—Biography—Juvenile literature. [1. Sacagawea, 1786–1884. 2.
  Shoshoni Indians—Biography. 3. Indians of North America—Biography. 4.
  Women—Biography. 5. Lewis and Clark Expedition (1804–1806)] I. Title.
  F592.7.S123 A48 2002
  978.004'9745'0092—dc21

                    2001007399

15   24   28

Contents

Chapter ONE	*A Young Shoshone Woman*	6
Chapter TWO	*Reaching the Columbia*	12
Chapter THREE	*Traveling Back*	18
Chapter FOUR	*Life after the Expedition*	24
	Time Line	29
	Glossary Terms	30
	For Further Information	31
	Index	32

A Young Shoshone Woman

SACAGAWEA (SAH-KUH-JUH-WEE-UH) WAS A young Shoshone woman who traveled with Meriwether Lewis and William Clark on their historic exploration of the American West. Their journey through the northwestern territory of the United States is often called the Lewis and Clark **expedition**. Sacagawea was the only woman on the trip. Because she took part in the expedition from 1805 to 1806, the Native Americans they met believed that they came in peace. War parties did not include women

This map shows Lewis and Clark's route, which began in St. Louis in 1804.

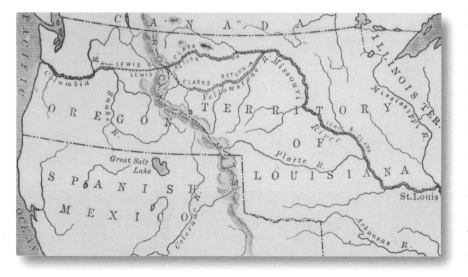

6

or children. Sacagawea also guided the expedition through land familiar to her.

The Lewis and Clark expedition set off from St. Louis in the fall of 1804. They carried clothing, tools, scientific books, medicine, rifles, and other goods. They took gifts for the Native Americans, such as beads, cotton cloth, ribbons, bells, and brass rings.

After sailing up the Missouri River, the expedition met the Mandan Indians in the Dakotas. They set up a winter camp and called it Fort Mandan.

Sacagawea joined the group when Lewis and Clark hired her husband, Toussaint Charbonneau, as an **interpreter**. Charbonneau was a French-Canadian fur trader. He was not known as an honest and capable man. However, he knew the

Fur traders like Charbonneau played an important part in opening the American West to settlement.

Interesting Fact

▸ Sacagawea's Shoshone name was *Bo-i-naiv* (BOH-ih-NY-eev).

7

A statue of Sacagawea with her son, Pomp, in Bismarck, North Dakota

language of the Indian peoples that Lewis and Clark expected to meet.

The fur trader was much older than his wife. Sacagawea was 16 or 17 years old. She was expecting a baby. In February 1805, she gave birth to a baby boy named Jean Baptiste. His nickname was Pomp, which means "first-born" in the Shoshone language.

Historians possess written information about Sacagawea's life between April 1805 and August 1806—her time with the Lewis and Clark expedition. All that is known about her earlier life comes from Shoshone **oral tradition**. The tribe had no written history.

Sacagawea was probably born to northern Shoshone people somewhere in Idaho. They were wandering people. Sacagawea learned the area's mountains and valleys on travels with her family.

When she was about 10 or 11 years old, Sacagawea's family traveled into Montana. Hidatsa Indians attacked their camp and kidnapped Sacagawea. She never spoke of her loneliness or unhappiness during this time, however. Then, Toussaint Charbonneau bought Sacagawea from the Hidatsa— or won her in a gambling game. These best guesses are all we know about this young Shoshone woman's life before the Lewis and Clark expedition.

Hidatsa Indians kidnapped Sacagawea when she was 10 or 11. This chief is a Hidatsa Indian.

IN 1803, THE UNITED STATES PURCHASED A HUGE AMOUNT OF LAND from France for $15 million. The Louisiana Purchase doubled the size of the country. Now the United States extended from the Mississippi River to the Rocky Mountains and from the Gulf of Mexico to the Canadian border (below). President Thomas Jefferson asked Congress to pay for an expedition to explore the land west of the Mississippi and Missouri Rivers.

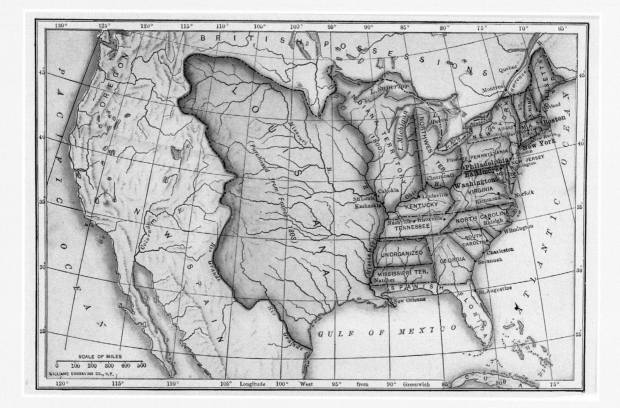

Jefferson asked Captain Meriwether Lewis to lead the expedition. Lewis had been a secretary to Jefferson and knew the West. He also knew how to live in the wilderness. Lewis chose a frontiersman named William Clark to lead the expedition with him. The group also included soldiers, frontiersmen, two boatmen, and Clark's slave, an African-American named York.

The Lewis and Clark expedition was the most important exploration in American history. They had to map the land. They also had to study the Native Americans they met as well as the plants, animals, fossils, and anything else they saw.

William Clark made many maps and sketches (such as the one above of a cock of the plains). Several members of the expedition kept journals and notebooks. These documents provided information for the first detailed maps of the American West and the Pacific Northwest.

Chapter TWO

Reaching the Columbia

WITH CHARBONNEAU, SACAGAWEA, AND Pomp, the expedition left Fort Mandan in April 1805. The party followed the Missouri River west to the mountains. They traveled on the water by **pirogue**. Sacagawea strapped her baby son on her back. She carried her belongings in a rawhide bag.

One day, a fierce storm blew their boat over on its side. Charbonneau was so frightened that he did not know what to do. But Sacagawea reacted calmly. She recovered the books and instruments that had floated out of the water. The expedition named that river after her. Today, it is known as Crooked Creek.

By May, they could see the Rocky Mountains. In June, they came to the Great Falls of the Missouri River. They built wagons

Sacagawea guided the expedition through land she knew.

to carry their boats and supplies around the falls. On one such **portage**, Sacagawea and Pomp were almost washed away in a flood.

The expedition reached the point where three rivers join to form the great Missouri. This place is called Three Forks. The travelers named the rivers the Madison, the Gallatin, and the Jefferson. They followed the Jefferson.

In the high country, Sacagawea recognized landmarks. She led the expedition into the mountains toward the **Continental Divide**. There the expedition met up with the Shoshone people.

Meriwether Lewis and William Clark meeting the Shoshone Indians

Sacagawea saw her people for the first time since the Hidatsa had kidnapped her. Sadly, most of her family had died. Two brothers and her sister's child were still alive.

One brother, Cameahwait, was the chief, and she greeted him joyfully. Following

Shoshone tradition, Sacagawea adopted her sister's son, Bazil. But she left the boy with his uncles.

Because Sacagawea was part of the expedition, the Shoshone sold them horses. They needed horses to cross the high Bitterroot Mountains. They crossed the Continental Divide to the Clearwater River. From there on, they could travel by boat.

The expedition bought horses from the Shoshone.

With Toussaint Charbonneau next to her, Sacagawea interprets for Lewis and Clark with Chinook Indians on the Columbia River.

The expedition followed the Clearwater River to the Snake River. Then they reached the Columbia River. In November 1805, they went down the beautiful Columbia River **Gorge**. The Columbia flows into the Pacific Ocean.

Columbia River Gorge as it looks today

SACAGAWEA IS OFTEN CALLED THE FIRST NATIVE AMERICAN heroine in history. But no one can decide on the spelling—or meaning—of her name. Should it be spelled *Sacagawea*, *Sacajawea*, or *Sakakawea*?

In their journals, Lewis and Clark spelled her name at least 14 different ways. William Clark once wrote of the river named after her, "This stream we called Sah-ca-gah-we-ah or 'bird woman's river,' after our interpreter—the snake woman." Later, William Clark gave Sacagawea the nickname "Janey." In the army at that time, the word *Jane* was slang for "girl."

Some northern Hidatsa insist the name is *Sakakawea*, but that name cannot be found in the Lewis and Clark journals. The Shoshone took the spelling *Sacajawea*. In their language, it means "boat launcher" or "boat pusher."

Journalists from the 1800s who wrote about the expedition spelled the name *Sacagawea*. As early as 1910, language experts made that the standard spelling.

Although Sacagawea was a Shoshone, the name goes back to the Hidatsa language. *Sacaga* means "bird," and *wea* means "woman." Thus she was the Bird Woman. One researcher suggests that we owe it to the country's most famous Native American woman to at least spell her name correctly.

Chapter THREE

Traveling Back

NEAR THE COAST OF THE PACIFIC OCEAN, the expedition built Fort Clatsop and stayed there for the winter. The local Indians were the Clatsop tribe. It was a difficult winter for everyone. For Christmas dinner, they had to eat badly spoiled elk and fish.

Visitors to Oregon can see this reproduction of Fort Clatsop.

Soon the Clatsop people reported that a huge whale had washed up on the shore of the Pacific Ocean. Sacagawea wanted to see the great ocean and the great animal. Clark took Sacagawea and

Charbonneau on a special trip to see the whale. But by the time they got there, all that was left were the bones. However, Clark bought some **blubber** from the Indians to use for oil.

The return trip was no easier than the journey out had been. The expedition members were often exhausted and nearly starved. Sacagawea helped by finding berries, nuts, and roots to eat.

Many expedition journals report that Sacagawea's cheerfulness encouraged the others. She proved to be much more helpful than her husband. Charbonneau could not ride horses well. He was uneasy and awkward in a pirogue. At least one time, Clark had to keep him from striking Sacagawea.

On the return journey to Fort Mandan, Lewis and Clark split up. Sacagawea and Charbonneau went south with Clark toward Yellowstone River.

Sacagawea was able to recognize an area where her tribe had dug roots. She assured Clark they were headed in the right direction. She also recommended trails that her tribe had followed. Clark wrote that she had been "of great service."

Interesting Fact

▸ A one-dollar coin commemorating Sacagawea went into circulation in the United States in 2000.

The group crossed the Continental Divide at Bozeman Pass. They reached the mouth of the Yellowstone. By August 14, 1806, they were back at Fort Mandan.

Sacagawea and Charbonneau stayed behind when Lewis and Clark left Fort Mandan. Charbonneau was paid about $500 for 16 months work. He also got two large canoes. Sacagawea received no payment.

Later, William Clark wrote Charbonneau from St. Louis. Clark had been fond of Pomp and Sacagawea. He offered to provide land and livestock for the family if Charbonneau wanted to live among the whites. He also offered to raise and educate Pomp.

Sometime between 1806 and 1810, Charbonneau accepted Clark's offer and traveled to St. Louis. It is not clear

William Clark's group crossed the Continental Divide at the Bozeman Pass.

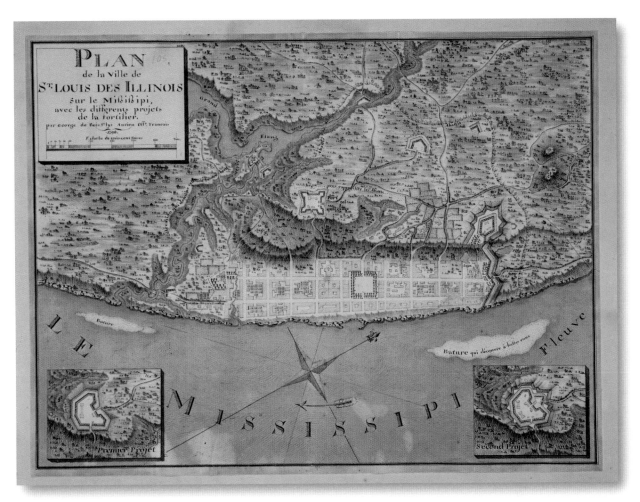

Toussaint Charbonneau traveled to St. Louis, shown in this 1796 map.

whether he took one or two Shoshone wives with him and one or two sons. If he took only one wife, it was surely Sacagawea.

Charbonneau bought land on the Missouri River from Clark, but sold it back in 1811. He wanted to return to life among the Native Americans and work at the fur trade. Charbonneau went north on the Missouri River with his Shoshone wife but without a son.

IN 1902, A WOMAN NAMED EVA EMERY DYE (left) published *The Conquest, The True Story of Lewis and Clark* (below, in a window display from 1903). The book drew public attention to the expedition and Sacagawea. Almost immediately, monuments went up to honor the Shoshone woman who had helped the expedition.

One statue was erected at the Louisiana Purchase Exposition in St. Louis in 1903. Another was put up at the Lewis and Clark Centennial Exposition in Portland, Oregon, in 1905. This statue shows Sacagawea holding Pomp and pointing westward (opposite).

22

Unfortunately, the sculptor did not realize Sacagawea was a young girl at the time. The statue shows an older woman. A speaker at the unveiling of the statue said that it spoke for many brave heroines who may have been overlooked by history.

In time, Sacagawea became a larger-than-life heroine. People believed that she alone had guided the expedition from Fort Mandan and back. Without her, the members of the expedition would surely have starved. Only her beauty outshone her survival and healing skills. Thus, Sacagawea became the subject of myth. While she played an important role on the expedition, there is no need to overstate her contributions.

Chapter FOUR

Life after the Expedition

Sacagawea's past is still largely unknown.

ACCORDING TO MANY HISTORIANS, SACAGAWEA died on December 20, 1812. She was at Fort Manuel in the Dakotas. Charbonneau was with a fur-trapping expedition that operated out of that fort. The fort's secretary made a record on that date. He wrote, "This evening the wife of Charbonneau, a Snake squaw, died of **putrid** fever. She was a good woman and the best woman in the fort, aged about 25 years. She left a fine infant girl."

It seems that the girl's name was Lizette. The secretary tried to adopt the baby. On the adoption papers, his name was scratched out, however, and replaced by William Clark's name. There is no other record of Lizette.

This photograph of Shoshone people standing near tepees was taken between 1880 and 1910.

Shoshone oral tradition tells a different story. According to that story, between 1850 and 1870, Sacagawea returned to Jean Baptiste, her adopted son Bazil, and the rest of her tribe. Jean Baptiste, who had returned to the tribe in 1829, didn't care much what happened to his mother. Bazil took good care of her, however.

The tribal elders respected this woman who called herself Sacagawea and spoke often of her experiences with Lewis and Clark. She adopted many of the white man's ways and encouraged the Shoshone to take up farming.

Several white men swore they had met this older Sacagawea. One government official who went to the reservation in 1871 claimed that a woman talked of traveling with Lewis and Clark and spoke English and French. She even described the huge whalebones on the beach. A young man at the Carlisle Indian School in Pennsylvania claimed that she was his great-grandmother. He said she had told him many stories of her life experience.

Historians have looked into the Shoshone story. Some believe that Charbonneau took two Snake or Shoshone wives and two sons to St. Louis after the expedition. He returned to the Dakotas with only one wife. These historians suggest that Sacagawea stayed behind with Jean Baptiste and Charbonneau's other son and later rejoined Charbonneau. He took a third wife but when that wife and Sacagawea did not get along, Sacagawea left him.

At one point, the story goes, she followed famous explorer John Charles Frémont to the northwest. Frémont made note of a Shoshone woman with his party in 1843. There are stories that she married several times and had more children.

No firm proof exists for either story about the end of Sacagawea's life, though. Written records suggest that she died in 1812. William Clark listed her as dead in his journal, which was made public in 1814. Most historians believe that Sacagawea was the only one who went to St. Louis and returned to the Dakotas.

So, who was the old woman of Shoshone oral tradition? She could have been a Shoshone who as a very young girl heard the real Sacagawea's adventures and repeated the stories as her own in old age. This old Shoshone woman, called Porivo by the tribe, died in 1884. Jean Baptiste died in 1885, and Bazil in 1886. Porivo is buried between the two men.

One story says that Sacagawea traveled with famous explorer John Charles Frémont in 1843.

27

▸ No photographs of Sacagawea exist. That fact strengthens the idea that she died in 1812. If she were alive in the late 1880s, surely we would have photographs of her.

Today, statues around the United States honor Sacagawea's efforts during the Lewis and Clark expedition. The country has named an island, a lake, a peak, and a mountain after Sacagawea. She was a woman of unusual capabilities, strength, and cheerfulness. She is rightly known as the first famous American Indian woman.

The grave of Sacagawea's son Jean Baptiste Charbonneau stands in Sacagawea Cemetery on a prairie in the Wind River Reservation in Wyoming.

c. 1788–1789 Sacagawea, a Shoshone, is born in northern Idaho.

c. 1798–1799 Sacagawea is kidnapped by the Hidatsa people.

1804 Sacagawea meets Meriwether Lewis and William Clark.

1805 Sacagawea gives birth to Pomp in February. In April, the expedition leaves Fort Mandan. In August, Sacagawea is reunited with the people of the Shoshone tribe. In November, the expedition reaches the Pacific Ocean.

1806 The expedition returns to Fort Mandan. Sacagawea and Charbonneau part company with Lewis and Clark.

c. 1806–1810 Charbonneau takes his family to St. Louis and buys farmland from Clark.

c. 1811–1812 Charbonneau sells his Missouri land back to Clark and takes his wife north, leaving his son behind with Clark.

1812 "The wife of Charbonneau" dies at Fort Manuel in the Dakotas.

c. 1850–1870 After many years of wandering, Sacagawea may have returned to her people. She is reunited with her son, Jean Baptiste, and her adopted son, Bazil.

1884 The Shoshone woman who called herself Sacagawea dies on the reservation.

1885 Baptiste dies.

1886 Bazil dies.

Glossary Terms

blubber (BLUH-bur)
Blubber is the fat under the skin of a whale. William Clark bought some blubber from Indians near the Pacific Ocean.

Continental Divide (KON-tuh-NEN-tull duh-VYD)
The Continental Divide is an imaginary line at the peaks of the Rocky Mountains. Rivers that lie west of the Continental Divide flow toward the Pacific Ocean. Rivers east of the divide flow toward the Gulf of Mexico, Hudson Bay, and the Arctic Ocean.

expedition (ek-spuh-DISH-uhn)
An expedition is a long journey made for a special purpose. President Thomas Jefferson asked Lewis and Clark to make an expedition to explore the northwest territory of the United States. An expedition can also be the group of people who make the journey.

gorge (GORJ)
A gorge is a deep valley with steep, rocky sides. The Lewis and Clark expedition traveled down the Columbia River Gorge in 1805.

interpreter (in-TUR-prit-er)
An interpreter is a person who translates for people who speak different languages. Charbonneau worked as an interpreter for Lewis and Clark.

oral tradition (OR-uhl truh-DISH-uhn)
Oral tradition is the handing down of history, beliefs, and customs through storytelling. Often it is the only history of people who have no written accounts. Since stories can change with each telling, it may be hard to know the truth of stories told in the oral tradition.

pirogue (pih-ROHG)
A pirogue is a canoe made from a tree trunk that has been hollowed out. The Lewis and Clark expedition traveled on the water by pirogue.

portage (POHR-tij)
Portage is the carrying of boats and supplies over land from one body of water to another, as in a waterfall.

putrid (PYOO-trid)
Something that is putrid is rotten or decaying. According to records, the wife of Charbonneau died of a putrid fever.

For Further INFORMATION

Web Sites

Visit our homepage for lots of links about Sacagawea:
http://www.childsworld.com/links.html

Note to Parents, Teachers, and Librarians:
We routinely verify our Web links to make sure they're safe,
active sites—so encourage your readers to check them out!

Books

Bruchac, Joseph. *Sacajawea: The Story of Bird Woman and the Lewis and Clark Expedition.* New York: Harcourt Silver Whistle Books, 2000.

Roop, Connie, and Peter Geiger Roop. *Girl of the Shining Mountains: Sacagawea's Story.* New York: Hyperion, 1999.

Rowland, Della. *The Story of Sacajawea, Guide to Lewis and Clark.* New York: Yearling Books, 1989.

St. George, Judith. *Sacagawea.* New York: Philomel Books, 1997.

Places to Visit or Contact

Lewis and Clark National Historic Trail Interpretive Center
To learn more about the Lewis and Clark expedition and the tribes of the Plains and the Pacific Northwest
4201 Giant Springs Road
P.O. Box 1806
Great Falls, MT 59403
406-727-8733

Sacajawea State Park and Interpretive Cente
To find out more about the story of Sacagawea
2503 Sacajawea Park Road
Pasco, WA 99301
509-545-2361

Index

Bazil (nephew), 15, 25, 28
Bitterroot Mountains, 15
Bozeman Pass, 20

Cameahwait (brother), 14
Charbonneau, Jean Baptiste "Pomp" (son),
    8, 12, 13, 20, 23, 25, 26, 28
Charbonneau, Lizette (daughter), 24
Charbonneau, Toussaint (husband), 7–8,
    9, 12, 19, 20, 21, 24, 26
Clark, William, 6, 11, 17, 19, 25, 26, 27
Clatsop tribe, 18
Clearwater River, 15, 16
Columbia River, 16
*The Conquest, The True Story of Lewis and
    Clark* (Eva Emery Dye), 22
Continental Divide, 13, 15, 20
Crooked Creek, 12

Fort Clatsop, 18
Fort Mandan, 7, 19, 20, 23
Fort Manuel, 24
Frémont, John Charles, 26–27
fur trade, 7, 12, 21

Gallatin River, 13
Great Falls, 12

Hidasta tribe, 9, 17

Jefferson River, 13
Jefferson, Thomas, 10–11

Lewis and Clark Centennial Exposition, 22–23
Lewis and Clark expedition, 6–7, 11
    Bitterroot Mountains, 15
    Bozeman Pass, 20
    Continental Divide, 13, 15, 20
    Crooked Creek, 12
    Fort Clatsop, 18
    Fort Mandan, 7, 19, 20, 23
    Gallatin River, 13
    Great Falls, 12
    Jefferson River, 13

journals, 11, 19, 27
    Madison River, 13
    Mandan tribe and, 7
    mapmaking, 11
    Missouri River, 12, 13
    Pacific Ocean, 18–19
    pirogues, 12, 19
    portages, 13
    Snake River, 16
    supplies, 7, 18, 19
    Thomas Jefferson and, 10–11
    Three Forks, 13
    Yellowstone River, 19
Louisiana Purchase, 10

Madison River, 13
Mandan tribe, 7
Missouri River, 12, 13
Montana, 9

Pacific Ocean, 18–19
Porivo (Shoshone woman), 28

Rocky Mountains, 12

Sacagawea
    Bazil (nephew) and, 15, 25, 28
    birth of, 9
    childhood of, 9
    coin, 19
    Crooked Creek and, 12
    death of, 24, 27
    kidnapping of, 9
    memorials to, 22–23, 28
    photographs of, 28
    Shoshone name, 7
    spelling of name, 17
Shoshone tribe, 6, 7, 8, 13–15, 17, 19–20,
    25–26, 27, 28
Snake River, 16

Three Forks, 13

Yellowstone River, 19